A Handbook of California
Personal Injury Law

Raymond J. Zolekhian, Esq.
Oakwood Legal Group, LLP

Copyright © 2018 by Raymond J. Zolekhian, Esq.

All rights reserved. No part of this publication may be reproduced, distributed, or transmitted in any form or by any means, including photocopying, recording, or other electronic or mechanical methods, without the prior written permission of the publisher, except in the case of brief quotations embodied in critical reviews and certain other noncommercial uses permitted by copyright law. For permission requests, write to the publisher, addressed "Attention: Permissions Coordinator," at the address below.

Speakeasy Publishing
73-03 Bell Blvd, #10
Oakland Gardens, NY 11364
www.speakeasypublishinginc.com

Ordering Information:

Quantity sales. Special discounts are available on quantity purchases by corporations, associations, and others. For details, contact the publisher at the address above.

Orders by U.S. trade bookstores and wholesalers. Please contact Speakeasy Publishing: Tel: (888) 991-2766 or visit www.speakeasypublishinginc.com.

Printed in the United States of America.

Published in 2018

ISBN: 978-1-946481-49-8

DISCLAIMER

This publication is intended to be used for educational purposes only. No legal advice is being given, and no attorney-client relationship is intended to be created by reading this material. The author assumes no liability for any errors or omissions or for how this book or its contents are used or interpreted or for any consequences resulting directly or indirectly from the use of this book. For legal or any other advice, please consult an experienced attorney or the appropriate expert who is aware of the specific facts of your case and is knowledgeable of the law in your jurisdiction.

Oakwood Legal Group
Attorneys at Law
Main Office – Los Angeles
470 S. San Vicente Blvd., Second Floor
Los Angeles, CA 90048
www.oakwoodlegal.com
310-205-2525

TESTIMONIALS

"Overall, I highly recommend the Oakwood Legal Team. They did everything in their power to make this process as easy as possible and were highly responsive to even the smallest of questions I had for them. I was hit by a drunk driver on the freeway and from the moment I first spoke with Raymond to describe the accident, the Oakwood team has exhibited the highest levels of professionalism. My case manager Fransheska worked as my point of contact through the process, and though the process took a very long time to settle, Fransheska did an excellent job of updating me every step of the way. She even went as far as to provide her cell phone number so we could text about the case. She responded to every question I had in a matter of hours (or less) and always quickly escalated questions that needed a response from one of the attorneys. I have a few friends who have been in similar accidents, and it seems like Oakwood's responsiveness and accessibility is rare. The whole team at Oakwood has been pleasure to work with. Ray and Michael were able to negotiate a great settlement amount and Matthew made the document management process very easy to deal with. The thing about Oakwood Legal is that they made the process feel so simple. They found a chiropractor that was around the corner from my apartment, were there to quickly answer any and every question I had, and have an e-signature system that saved so much time. Because these cases can take time, it's little things like that that make all the difference. While I hope I never get into another car accident, if I do, I wouldn't consider working with anyone other than Oakwood Legal."

- Steven R.

****

"I have to say that this group was the MOST responsive law firm I have ever worked with. They are top professionals, courteous and have an extreme attention to detail. I needed something quickly and they came to my rescue and exceeded my expectations. Needless to say, I will be using them again. Do not hesitate to contact, you will not be disappointed. All injury law firms should strive to be this well managed. My best wishes to them for continued success in everything they do. New Fan P.S. special thanks to Mike and Ray! You guys rock! Thanks for having my back!"

- Eli B.

****

"If you have been involved in an accident and are not sure what to do...you have to call Oakwood Legal Group. Their entire team is outstanding. I was rear-ended in LA as I was completely stopped at a red light. From the very outset I felt as if I was in excellent hands from my initial consultation, with them taking over and dealing with the insurance companies and assisting with getting me the medical treatment I needed to help me recover. Matthew is great. Fransheska is an amazing case worker. And most importantly...Raymond Zolekhian is just about as good as it gets when it comes to your attorney stepping up and fighting to get you what you deserve. Everything that they discussed with me was honest and true! I strongly suggest you give them a call if you've been in an accident and get them on your side immediately."

- Todd S.

****

"I don't give out reviews unless I know they helped me… but my lawyer Raymond was unbelievable and his partner Mike was such a great help in winning my case. If you cannot find a good lawyer and if you believe you have a good case, don't hesitate to give them a call… trust me you won't regret it. Good smart lawyers like Raymond and his partner Mike … Thank you again, guys."

- Veronica C.

****

"This review is long overdue. This is truly the BEST legal team you could ever have on your side. When I was in my accident I was frustrated and lost with the process as the insurance company was quickly working to give me as little compensation for my losses as possible. I sent a request for information with Oakwood Legal and although it was after traditional business hours I was contacted almost immediately and my questions were being answered right away. They took my case, sent me to the medical professionals to help me with my injuries and in the end won a settlement that was much much more than I thought possible! Anytime I had a question they were always there to quickly answer them. I don't know what I would have done without this team! Thank you all so much!! If you are looking for an attorney, stop your search and call them right away!"

- **LaKendra C.**

****

"Everyone at Oakwood Legal Group was a big help with my case. I was very happy they were there for me in the beginning to the end of my case. If I ever need Oakwood Legal Group, I would do it again."

- **Kathy M.**

****

TABLE OF CONTENTS

i.	Disclaimer	3
ii.	Testimonials	5
iii.	About The Author	10
1.	Personal Injury Cases That Oakwood Legal Group Handles	13
2.	Things to Do After an Injury	16
3.	Defenses Insurance Companies Use to Avoid Paying Claims	19
4.	What to Expect After A Claim Is Filed?	23
5.	How Does Going to Trial Affect Costs of Injury Process?	25
6.	Personal Injury Process	28
iv.	What Is The Next Step?	42
v.	Index	43
vi.	Notes	45

About The Author

Raymond Zolekhian was born and raised in Los Angeles. He attended Beverly Hills High School, UCLA (B.A. in Business Economics, magna cum laude) and Harvard Law School. He got his first job at a law firm when he was 14 years old. After graduating from Harvard, he was hired as an attorney in the Los Angeles office of Skadden, Arps, Slate, Meagher and Flom, LLP, a law firm with over 1,700 attorneys in 22 offices around the world. The Financial Times names Skadden the most innovative law firm in North America. His clients at Skadden included the NBA, El Pollo Loco, IHOP and many other major corporations.

After 3 years at Skadden, he left to start his own law firm so that he could help the average person rather than major corporations. Since starting his own practice, he has been named as one of the Top 100 Trial Lawyers and The Top 40 Under 40 by The National Trial Lawyers, a Rising Star by Super Lawyers Magazine from 2014-2018 and has obtained 10.0 AVVO Rating. He has also been admitted to the Million Dollar and Multi-Million Dollar Advocates Forum.

He has featured in The Los Angeles Times, The Beverly Hills Weekly, The National Law Journal and Law360.com. He has received numerous million and multi-million dollar verdicts and settlements including a $4.1 million verdict in 2014 on a slip and fall case and was named by VerdictSearch as one of the 10 largest slip and fall verdicts in the entire state of California.

CHAPTER 1

PERSONAL INJURY CASES THAT OAKWOOD LEGAL GROUP HANDLES

Attorney Raymond Zolekhian handles truck accidents, motorcycle accidents, wrongful death, brain injuries, Uber/Lyft accidents, auto accidents, bicycle accidents, pedestrian accidents, slip and falls, trip and falls, uninsured motorist claims, and dog bites.

Misunderstandings About Working with A Personal Injury Attorney

People often think that all personal injuries do is take a portion of the settlement. They don't realize how much value we add. Here are some examples: On a trip and fall brain injury case, the insurance company's maximum offer before trial was $225,000 and we were able to get the client $4.1 million; on a case where a mechanic didn't properly inspect a tire on a vehicle that caused a car accident injuring our client, the mechanic's insurance company was offering no money for over a year until we were able to get a $1 million settlement; on a rear end case where my client had to receive a back surgery, for almost one year the insurance company's maximum offer was $100,000 and we went to arbitration and got the client $915,000.

What Sets Your Firm Apart in Handling Personal Injury Cases?

Our lawyers have been trained at some of the top law schools in the country, including Harvard and UCLA. That training combined with our decades of experience gives us the edge over other personal injury attorneys and insurance company lawyers. Our attorneys have been trained from day one to think outside the box and see unique ways to create value in a case that most other attorneys will not see. We use our knowledge to outsmart, outthink and outmaneuver insurance company defense attorneys to get results for our clients that other attorneys can't get.

CHAPTER 2

THINGS TO DO AFTER AN INJURY

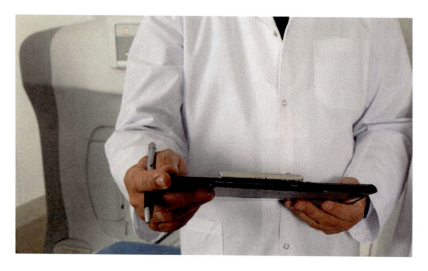

You should seek medical treatment as soon as possible so that a doctor can document your injuries and provide you with recommendations on how to get better.

Danger of Waiting Too Long for Medical Treatment

One of the biggest mistakes that people make is waiting days, weeks or even months before seeking medical treatment for their injuries. This is one of the biggest obstacles to recovering from your injuries and to getting a good settlement. There are a number of legitimate reasons why someone might wait to seek medical treatment. It could be a result of not having health insurance, not having money, not being able to take time off of work, not having access to a doctor or just hoping that the pain will go away with time. Now while all these are legitimate reasons, waiting to see a doctor allows insurance companies to make the argument that either you weren't as hurt as you say you were in the accident or that something other than the accident was a cause of your injury.

Follow Doctor's Advice

By not following the doctor's recommendation or by missing medical appointments, it allows the insurance company to make the argument that you're not as injured as you say you are.

Gap in Care and How It affects A Claim

A gap in care is a time period of typically weeks or months where you don't see a doctor for your injuries. Again, this allows insurance companies to make the argument that either you weren't as hurt as you say you were in the accident or that something other than the accident was a cause of your injury.

Misconceptions About Recovery Process

People believe that insurance companies are there to help them in their time of need. The exact opposite is true. Insurance companies are in business to make large profits. They make hundreds of billions of dollars in profits each year. They do that by taking in insurance premiums each and every month, and not paying out claims. Insurance companies use every excuse they can in order to not pay your claim or give you less than you deserve. They will argue you are lying about your injuries or that that medical treatment you received wasn't necessary, all in an effort to pay you less than they should. We know all their tricks and can fight through their lies to get you what you deserve.

CHAPTER 3

DEFENSES INSURANCE COMPANIES USE TO AVOID PAYING CLAIMS

Insurance companies say the accident wasn't strong enough to cause an injury. The injury that the client is suffering from was pre-existing. The client isn't as injured as they are claiming. The medical treatment that client received wasn't necessary.

What Does an Attorney Need Before Filing A Claim?

The attorney needs facts of how the accident happened, what injuries you are suffering from and any photos of the accident.

Damages an Injured Person Should Seek

You are entitled to recover for past and future medical expenses, past and future loss of earnings, and past and future pain and suffering. Insurance companies will fight each and every one of these claims so it is important that all your injuries and expenses are properly documented. Without the proper proof, the insurance company will deny the claims.

What Will Reimbursement Include?

Reimbursement will include medical bills already paid, as well as for future medical treatment that will be necessary. But typically, you can get a greater recovery for past medical expenses than you can for future medical expenses.

As far as providers or sources of funds that are entitled to and will typically recoup reimbursement once a settlement is achieved, they are medical providers, health insurance companies, Medicare, Medi-cal and workers compensation insurance carriers are all entitled to recoup reimbursement from a settlement.

Does Having A Lawyer Involved Make Insurance Companies Evaluate Your Claim Differently?

Insurance companies operate out of fear and they are scared of only one thing. The only thing they fear is the possibility of having to go trial and being subject to a large verdict. That fear is only triggered once there is a lawyer involved. Without an attorney being involved, the insurance company has no fear of trial so they don't fairly evaluate the claim. We understand how to use various legal tools to increase their fear factor and put pressure on them to pay maximum dollar to our clients.

The threat of going to trial enhances the likelihood of a larger settlement from insurance companies. An attorney's trial or negotiating skills play an important role in how the insurance company evaluates a case and what they offer as a settlement. Insurance companies are constantly evaluating the personal injury attorneys that they are going up against. They know the good ones and they know the bad ones. Insurance companies are aware that our attorneys have decades of experience, have successfully handles thousands of cases including numerous trials, and were trained at some of the top law schools in the country including Harvard. They know that we will do whatever is necessary to get the best outcome for our clients.

Chapter 4

What to Expect After a Claim Is Filed?

Once we are hired as your attorneys, we will handle all communications with the other side. This will allow you to focus on recovering from your injuries and not have to deal with the stress of dealing with insurance companies. This also allows us to ensure that everything is being handled properly in an effort to get you the best outcome possible.

Factors That Lead A Case to Litigation

Any one or a combination of the following factors leads a case to litigation: disputes as to who is at fault, disputes as to the seriousness of your injuries, disputes as to the necessity of your medical treatment, disputes as the amount of your loss of earnings, disputes as to the severity of your pain and suffering.

What to Expect If Your Case Goes to Trial?

Trial is a rare, but necessary, occurrence. Trial occurs when the gap between what we believe is a fair settlement for our client and what the insurance company is offering is so large that the potential benefits of trial outweigh the costs and risks. As a result of budget cuts, courthouse are extremely backed up. As a result, getting to trial can take well over a year from the time a lawsuit is filed. The length of the trial itself depends on the complexity of the case. It can take anywhere from one weeks to several months.

CHAPTER 5

HOW DOES GOING TO TRIAL AFFECT COSTS OF INJURY PROCESS?

Going to trial significantly increases the costs of the personal injury process. That is why we will only recommend going to trial if we believe that the increased recovery that we might be able to get in trial is much greater than the increased costs. We will only recommend going to trial if we believe that it will put more money in our client's pocket. This is a decision that's only made after we discuss the pros and cons of trial with our client so that our client can make an informed decision.

If the insurance company and your attorney agree upon a settlement, it will usually take anywhere from a few weeks to a few months to get the settlement amount depending on the complexity of the case and number of medical providers that need to be paid.

There are some simple tips that will potentially help your case. Always be honest with your attorney and follow their instructions. See a doctor as soon as the accident occurs and make sure to tell them about all of your body parts that are causing you pain. Don't miss doctor and therapy appointments. Follow all of your doctor's recommendations for treatment. Continue with your medical treatment until your doctor has discharged you from care. Make all social media private.

Can I Afford A Highly Experienced Personal Injury Attorney?

We work on a contingency fee basis so we only get paid if we can get you a settlement. You will never have to pay our firm anything out of pocket. If we don't get you a settlement, you don't owe us anything.

Advice for Clients Who Think They Can Handle Their Case on Their Own

Just like in a criminal case where getting a great attorney can be the difference between going to jail and going home, having a great attorney in a personal injury case can be the difference between getting lots of money in your pocket and going home empty handed. While a personal injury case may seem simple, there are a lot of moving parts that need to be working in coordination with each other in order for your recovery to be maximized. There is the preservation of evidence, the documentation of injuries, the coordination of medical treatment and factoring in the various insurance policy limits just to name a few. Our team of attorneys come to the office day and day out to make sure that the moving parts are all working together on every case. Without an experienced personal injury attorney handling all these moving parts, one wrong move can cost you our entire settlement.

Chapter 6

Personal Injury Process

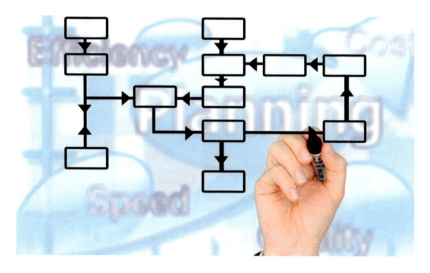

1. Do people generally underestimate the personal injury claim process?

People think that the insurance company is there to help them. They believe that simply because they were in an accident, especially if the insurance company has accepted liability or fault, that everything will be taken care. Insurance companies, however, make their money by paying out as little as possible on claims. Insurance companies will try to argue that the injuries couldn't have been caused by the accident or that the injuries are not as severe as they actually are. These and countless other arguments are used to reduce the amount that they insurance company has to pay. We have experience in not only fighting these arguments, but making sure that everything is properly documented from day1 so that we have the proper evidence to prove our clients' claims.

2. What documents and information should I be gathering to begin the claim process? What can my attorney help with?

Photos are extremely important. If you were in an auto accident, safely try to take photos of both the vehicle that you were in and the vehicle of the other party. If you were involved in a slip and fall, take photos of what caused you to fall. If your injuries are visible, take photos of your injuries. These photos can be extremely important is helping us prove your case. Especially in the case of a trip and fall, we can quickly send out an expert who can take photos of the scene and measurements before the area is repaired.

3. What factors make a sound and viable personal injury claim vs. one that isn't going to get anywhere?

Having a good liability argument is the first step in a viable personal injury claim. If we can make a strong case that the defendant was negligent, then we are off to a great start. The value of the case will depend on other factors, such as the significance of the injuries, but a good liability case always sets your case off in the right direction.

4. How long do personal injury cases typically take on average to be resolved?

The length of your case will generally depend on the length of your medical treatment and whether or not the insurance company is being reasonable in settlement negotiations. In almost all cases, it is best to wait until your medical treatment is complete before beginning settlement negotiations. That way we can make sure we are getting you full value for your injuries. If the insurance company is being unreasonable with their settlement offers, that will force us to file a lawsuit which may cause the case to take longer to resolve. However, we will only recommend filing a lawsuit if we believe that it can get you a much better outcome. The typical case takes about 9 months to resolve.

Fault/Likelihood of Collecting

5. What if I was not wearing a seat belt at the time of my accident? Or what if I was ticketed for something else? Can I still recover damages?

Yes, you can still recover damages, however the amount of your damages may be reduced. California is what is called a Comparative Liability state. What that means is that even if you are partly at fault for the accident, you can still recover damages. Your damages will be reduced by whatever percentage you are found to be at fault.

6. What role does the police report play in my personal injury claim after an auto accident?

A police report can be important in helping determine the facts of the case, however it is not legally considered evidence and is not admissible in court. So while a favorable police report can give your case a big boost, simply being found to be at fault on a police report doesn't automatically mean that you don't have a case.

7. Can I still win my case if my memory now conflicts with things I might have said at the time of the accident?

Memories can change over time as events in the distant past are oftentimes not as easily remembered as when they are fresh in your head. While it may make the case more difficult, you can still win your case if your memory now conflicts with what you may have said at the time of the accident. What is most important is that you are being truthful at all times.

8. In an auto accident, what happens if the at fault driver is in his or her company vehicle when the car accident occurs? Who will pay for my injuries?

In this scenario the insurance company for the company will typically cover the claim. This usually works out in your favor because company vehicle's generally carry much larger insurance policies.

9. In an auto accident, if the at-fault driver was borrowing someone else's car, who will pay for my injuries and the damage to my vehicle?

Depending on the circumstances, either the insurance company for the vehicle owner, the insurance company for the driver and in some situations both insurance companies, will pay for your damages. If neither of them have insurance, your Uninsured Motorist Coverage will pay for your damages. If you do not have Uninsured Motorist Coverage, you should contact your insurance company immediately and look into adding it to your policy. It is one of the most important coverages you can have.

Medical

10. What information should I share with my medical doctor? Can that information be used against me?

You should always be truthful with your medical providers. You should not exaggerate your injuries, but at the same time you should not downplay them either.

11. If the other party's insurance adjuster or other employee contacts me, what should I do?

It is always best to have an attorney handle all communications with any of the parties involved, whether it's an insurance adjuster, the other party or witness. Insurance adjusters will almost always records any conversation that you have with them. They then use any innocent inconsistencies between one statement you made to them and another statement you may make down the road in an effort to portray you as being dishonest. We will rarely ever allow our clients to speak directly to an insurance adjuster.

12. Should I ever release my medical records to any insurance adjuster?

What most people don't know is that insurance adjusters are legally entitled to only a very limited set of your medical records, but when they ask you to sign a release allowing them to access your medical records, they typically get to access everything. Our firm handles providing medical records to the insurance company and we make sure that they see only what they are legally entitled to see and nothing more.

13. What is an independent medical examination?

Only in cases where a lawsuit is filed does the insurance company have the right to perform an independent medical examination. The process involves a doctor hired by the insurance company performing an examination of you to determine the extent of your injuries. In reality, there is nothing independent about this. Until very recently, this was actually (and more appropriately) called a defense medical examination. This is a doctor hired and paid for by the insurance company in an effort to minimize the extent of your injuries and reduce the amount of your recovery. We will always hire a trained nurse to accompany our clients to this medical examination to make sure that our client feel prepared, comfortable and to ensure that the doctor asks only the questions that he is legally permitted to ask.

14. Do you advise I keep a diary or journal of what happened in the accident, what doctors I visit? Why or why not?

It is a good idea to keep a journal that will help you remember what type of daily difficulties the injuries had caused you.

Settlement

15. How are the settlement amounts calculated?

You are entitled to recover for the following 6 different categories of damages: 1. Past Medical Expense; 2. Future Medical Expenses; 3. Past Loss of Earning; 4. Future Loss of Earnings; 5. Past Pain and Suffering; 6. Future Pain and Suffering. The burden of proof is on us as the plaintiff's attorney to prove the amount of these damages and the insurance companies use every trick in the book to try to lower or eliminate these damages. If you as the plaintiff in an accident where you are driving a vehicle and you don't have liability insurance, you are generally prohibited by law from recovering past and future pain and suffering. It doesn't mean that you still don't have a good case, but it does mean that the amount of your potentially recovery is greatly reduced. This is another reason why it is important to always be insured.

16. How do you calculate pain and suffering?

Pain and suffering is an extremely difficult concept to put a monetary value on. Oftentimes, this is the category of damages where there is the most disagreement between us and the insurance companies. Our over 50 years of combined experience and having handled thousands of cases has given us the knowledge to determine what is a reasonable amount for pain and suffering based on the facts of each individual case.

17. Does the severity of the injury, ensure the likelihood of a larger settlement?

There are many factors that determine the size of the settlement, but generally a more severe injury has the potential for a larger settlement.

18. Will have preexisting conditions impact the amount of my settlement or chances of getting any settlement?

Preexisting conditions are one the insurance companies most frequently used arguments in attempting to reduce the settlement amount that they offer. As a result, preexisting conditions oftentimes complicate a case, however we have dealt with thousands of cases where our clients have had preexisting conditions so we know how to effectively address this issue and ensure that our clients still get a large settlement.

19. Should I apply for disability benefits and how can that affect a settlement?

If your doctor is putting you on disability, then Applying for disability will not affect your settlement.

20. What role might a forensic economic expert's role in a claim?

In cases where there is a large future loss of earnings claim, a forensic economic expert can help accurately calculate the value of that claim.

21. Are medical bills always going to be paid in full in a settlement?

In almost all the cases that we handle, medical bills will be paid in a full in a settlement. There are a few unique cases where based on the amount and type of medical bills and the amount of available insurance, it is difficult to pay for all the bills. We always do our best to make sure that all medical bills are paid for and our client walks away with a significant amount of the settlement in their pocket.

22. Is it generally a good idea to try and pay my medical bills as they come in, or should I wait until a settlement is reached?

We treat each bill on a case by case basis. Oftentimes, we are able to negotiate a deal with the medical provider to put the bill on hold until the case settled. However, if you are concerned about a bill going to collections, it is always best to pay it as soon as possible.

23. Does that mean that my settlement will essentially be all used to pay for medical bills and attorney fees, meaning there will not be much left over?

In almost all of our cases our clients will take home at least 1/3 of the total settlement amount. In many cases, they took home much more than that.

24. Why should I settle my claim? Is that usually better than going to trial?

Settling a case provides the advantage of having certainty as to the amount that you will get. It also allows the process to end more quickly and eliminates the need of having to put your life on hold for sometimes weeks at a time to attend a trial. In some cases, however, the insurance company is being so unreasonable with their settlement offers, that taking the case to trial is the only way to try to obtain a just resolution to your case.

25. Is there a minimum personal injury settlement amount which must be offered?

No. The insurance company has no duty to you that requires them to make a minimum settlement offer.

26. Can I reject a settlement offer?

The decision is always up to the client as to whether or not they want accept or reject a settlement. It is our job to try to get the maximum settlement offer on the table and give you our best advice, based on our decades of experience, as to whether or not we believe the settlement offer should be accepted.

27. How do you know, as the attorney, when it is time to accept an offer?

Having handled thousands of cases, we have a very good understanding of what the potential upside and downside of a case is and if we feel that the potential downside of a case is greater than the potential upside, then it is the right time to settle.

28. How are personal injury settlements paid out?

Personal injury settlements are paid out in one lump sum to our law firm. The funds are placed in our Client Trust Account and then distributed from there to the medical providers, law firm and the client.

WHAT IS THE NEXT STEP?

Visit www.oakwoodlegal.com or call us at 888-804-7858 to evaluate your claim.

INDEX

A

ARBITRATION · 14

B

BURDEN OF PROOF · 36

C

CLAIM · 21
COMPARATIVE LIABILITY STATE · 31
CONTINGENCY FEE BASIS · 26
CRIMINAL CASE · 27

F

FORENSIC ECONOMIC EXPERT · 38

H

HEALTH INSURANCE · 17

I

INNOCENT INCONSISTENCIES · 34
INSURANCE ADJUSTER · 34

L

LIABILITY INSURANCE · 36
LOSS OF EARNINGS · 20

M

MAXIMUM SETTLEMENT OFFER · 41

P

PAIN AND SUFFERING · 20
PERSONAL INJURY PROCESS · 25
PREEXISTING CONDITIONS · 38

R

REAR END CASE · 14

S

SETTLEMENT · 14

T

TRIAL · 14

U

UNINSURED MOTORIST COVERAGE · 33

NOTES

Made in the USA
Las Vegas, NV
14 May 2024

89907066R00029